The Heart of Inspiration

BRENDA LOZADA

Brenda Lozada
The Heart of Inspiration

All rights reserved
Copyright © 2024 by **Brenda Lozada**

Published by Spines
ISBN: 979-8-89383-015-6

This book is dedicated to those who seek to accept Jesus Christ as LORD and Savior. And desire to have a heart to please and serve him.

To my grandchildren: Jaleel Crater, Laila Braimah, Jahzara Carter, Kiaro Braimah, Kadir Braimah, Jasira Carter, Kamal Braimah. You can do anything you put your mind to just know that with God all things are possible.

Contents

Chapter One

FEAR

Fear thou not: I am with thee; be not dismayed; for I and thy God; I will strengthen thee; yea I will help thee; yea I will uphold thee with thy right hand of my righteousness.

— ISAIAH 41:10

Pray and Reflect on the verse. In what ways does this verse apply to your life right now? How can you overcome fear?

Faults, Evidence, Appearing, Real.

Chapter Two

FAITH

Now faith is the substance of things hoped for, the
evidence of things not seen

— HEBREWS 11:1

How does faith help you when you go thru hard times?
Why having faith is so important?

Chapter Three

SADNESS

Jehovah is close to the brokenhearted; he saves those who are crushed in spirit.

— PSALM 34:18

God promises to support you when you feel sad. Why is sadness important? How does sadness help in life?

Chapter Four

JOY

And the ransomed of the Lord shall return, and come to Zion with songs, and everlasting joy upon their heads: they shall obtain joy and gladness, and sorrow and sighing shall flee away.

— ISAIAH 35:10

Pray and Reflect on this verse. In what ways does this verse apply to you in your life right now? How do you describe joy? What situations in your life allow you to feel joy?

Chapter Five

LOVE

Let all that you do be done in love.

— 1 CORINTHIANS 14:16

Pray and Reflect on the verse. In what ways does this verse apply to you in your life? How important is it to love?

Chapter Six

MERCY

But God, who is rich in mercy, for his great love wherewith he loved us. Vs 5 Even when we were dead in sin, he has quickened us together, he loved us.

— EPHESIANS 2 :4-5

Pray and Reflect on this verse. In what ways does this verse apply to your life right now? How can we show mercy to someone that has hurt or done wrong toward you? Is it important to be and show mercy?

Chapter Seven

LONELINESS

For he satisfies the longing soul, and filleth the hungry soul with goodness.

— PSALM 107 :9

Pray and Reflect on this verse. In what ways does this verse apply to your life? In what ways can you handle being lonely?

What's the spiritual root of loneliness?

Chapter Eight

KINDNESS

For his merciful kindness is great toward us: and the truth of the Lord endureth forever. Praise Ye the Lord

— PSALM 117:2

Pray and Reflect on this verse. In what ways does this verse apply to your life? What is kindness and how do you show it?

What is the spiritual principle of kindness?

Chapter Nine

GRATITUDE

For every creature of God is good, and nothing to be refused, if it be received with thanksgiving.

— 1 TIMOTHY 4:4

Pray and reflect on this verse. In what ways does this verse apply to your life right now? What is the true meaning of gratitude?

Chapter Ten

CONFIDENCE

In the fear of the Lord is strong confidence and his children shall have a place of refuge.

— PSALM 14:26

Pray and reflect on the verse. In what ways does this verse apply to your life right now? How would you define confidence?

Chapter Eleven

JEALOUSY

And Joshua said unto the people, Ye cannot serve the Lord: for he is an holy God; he is a jealous God; he will not forgive your transgressions nor your sins. Vs 20 If ye forsake the LORD and serve strange gods, then he will turn and do you hurt, and consume you, after that he hath done you good.

— JOSHUA 24:19-20

Pray and reflect on this verse. In what ways does jealousy present itself to you? How do you handle it?

Why is God a jealous God?

Chapter Twelve

COURAGE

Be strong and of good courage, fear not nor be afraid of
the LORD THY GOD, he it is that doth go with thee, he
will not fail thee nor forsake thee.

— DEUTERONOMY 31:6

Pray and reflect on this verse. In what ways does courage
benefit one's life? What is a courageous person?

What is the true meaning of courage? Why is courage
important to God?

Chapter Thirteen

GENTLENESS

Blessed are the meek: for they shall inherit the earth.

— MATTHEW 5:5

Pray and reflect on the verse. What does gentleness mean? What does gentleness look like?

What are the equalities of gentleness?

Chapter Fourteen

ANGER

Be ye angry, and sin not: not the sun go down upon
your wrath.

— EPHESIANS 4:26

Pray and Reflect on the verse. In what ways does this
verse apply to your life? What causes anger? How do you
handle being angry?

Chapter Fifteen

COMPASSION

It is the LORD's mercies that we are not consumed,
because his compassion fails not.

— LAMENTATION 3:22

Pray and Reflect on this verse. What is compassion? What
are ways you can show compassion? Why is compassion
important?

Chapter Sixteen

PEACE & INNER CALM

And the peace of God, which passeth all understanding, shall keep your hearts and minds through Christ Jesus.

— PHILIPPIANS 4:7

Pray and Reflect on this verse. What does peace mean? How can you strengthen your inner calm regardless of circumstances that come in your life?

Chapter Seventeen

GUILT

If we confess our sins, he is faithful and just and will forgive us our sins and purify us from all unrighteousness.

— 1 JOHN 1:9

Pray and Reflect on this verse. What is guilt? How can guilt bring about a change in your life?

What is the feeling of guilt? What does guilt mean?

Chapter Eighteen

PATIENCE

And the LORD will direct your heart into the love of God, and into the patient waiting for Christ.

— 2 THESSALONIANS 3:5

Pray and Reflect on this verse. What does patience mean?

Chapter Nineteen

~~~

CARE

Cast all your care upon him for he careth for you.

— 1 PETER 5:7

Pray and Reflect on this verse. In what ways does this verse apply to your life right now.

Chapter Twenty

HATRED

He that hideth hatred with lying lips, and he that utters slander is a fool.

— PROVERB 10:18

Pray and Reflect on this verse.What's the difference between hate and hatred.What does God say about hate in your heart?

Chapter Twenty-One

OVERCOMER

To him that overcometh will I grant to sit with me on
my throne, even as I also overcome, and am set down
with my father on his throne.

— REVELATION 3:21

Pray and Reflect on this verse. How do you know if you are
an Overcomer? What have you overcame situations in
your life ?

Chapter Twenty-Two

DEPRESSION

The LORD is high unto them that are of a broken heart;
and saveth such as are of a contrite spirit.

— PSALM 34:18

Pray and Reflect on this verse. Can peace of mind be a remedy to combat depression? What are the ways to address depression?

Chapter Twenty-Three

STRONG

Have I not commanded you? Be strong and
courageous. Do not be afraid; do not be discouraged,
for the Lord your God will be with you wherever
you go.

— THE SONG OF SOLOMON 8:6

Pray and Reflect on this verse. In what ways can you be
strong? With the help of God how can we stand strong
in him?

What is the meaning behind being strong? Can you be
strong in God? How?

Chapter Twenty-Four

WEAK

But God has chosen the foolish things of the world

To confound the wise, and God hath chosen the weak things of the world to confound the things which are mighty.

— 1 CORINTHIANS 1:27

Pray and Reflect on this verse. In what ways does this verse apply to your life? What does weak stand for?

What does God do when we are weak?

Chapter Twenty-Five

GOODNESS

Surely goodness and mercy shall follow me all the days of my life and I will dwell in the house of the LORD forever.

— PSALM 23:6

Pray and Reflect on this verse. In what ways does this verse apply to your life? What does goodness mean?

Give a few examples of God's goodness that happen in your life.

Chapter Twenty-Six

DOUBT

Jesus answered and said unto them, Verily I say unto you If you have faith and doubt not, ye shall not only do this which is done to the fig tree, but also if ye shall say unto the mountain, Be thou removed, and be thou cast into the sea; it shall be done.

— MATTHEW 21:21

Pray and Reflect on this verse. In what ways does this verse apply to your life? What does doubt mean? Why is it not good to doubt God?

Chapter Twenty-Seven

GIVING

Give, and it shall be given unto you, good measure, pressed down and shaken together, and running over, shall men give into your bosom, for with the same measure that ye mete withal it shall be measured to you again.

— LUKE 6:38

Pray and Reflect on this verse. In what ways can you give? What is the purpose of giving? What does giving mean to you?

What is the act of giving? Can giving me offered in other ways? Give examples.

Chapter Twenty-Eight

TRUST

Trust in the LORD with all thine heart; and lean not unto thine own understanding. In all thy ways acknowledge Him, he shall direct thy paths.

— PROVERD 3 5-6

Pray and Reflect on this verse. In what ways does this verse apply to your life? What does trust mean? How can we show God that he can be trusted?

What is the true meaning of trust? What happens when trust is broken?

Chapter Twenty-Nine

FORGIVING

Forbearing one another, and forgiving one another, if any man have a quarrel against any; even Christ forgave you, so also do ye.

— THE COLOSSIANS 3:13

Pray and Reflect on this verse. In what ways does this verse apply to your life? What does forgiving mean? How do you handle forgiving someone when they did you wrong?

Chapter Thirty

SYMPATHY

For we do not have a high priest who cannot sympathize with our weakness, but One who has been tempted in all things as we are, yet without sin.

— HEBREWS 4:15

Pray and Reflect on this verse. In what ways does this verse apply to you in your life? What does sympathy mean to you? Does Jesus still show us sympathy?

Chapter Thirty-One

PITY

Like as a father pitieth his children so the LORD pitieth
them that fear him.

— PSALM 103: 13

Pray and Reflect on this verse. What does pity mean? How
does pity relate to grace?

Chapter Thirty-Two

HAPPINES

Behold God is my salvation; I will trust, and will not be
afraid; for the Lord God is my strength and my song,
and he has become my salvation.

— ISAIAH 12:2

Pray and Reflect on this verse. What does happiness
mean?How can I share God's happiness?

Chapter Thirty-Three

GRACE

For the LORD God is a sun and shield; the LORD will give grace and glory: no good thing will he withhold from them that walk uprightly.

— PSALM 84: 11

Pray and Reflect on this verse. What is grace? What is God's grace?

Chapter Thirty-Four

DILLIGENCE

Keep thy heart with all diligence; for out of it are the issues of life.

— PROVERBS 4:23

Pray and Reflect on this verse. What is the meaning of diligence? What are the benefits of diligence?

Chapter Thirty-Five

COVETOUSNESS

And he said to them. Take heed and beware of covetousness for a man's life consisteth not in the abundance of the things which he possesseth.

— LUKE 12:15

Pray and Reflect on this verse. What does covetousness mean? What types of covetousness are there?

Chapter Thirty-Six

SELFISH

Let nothing be done through strife or vain glory; but in lowliness of mind let each esteem others better than themselves. Look not every man at his own things, but every man also at the things of others.

— PHILIPPIANS 2: 3-4

Pray and Reflect on this verse. What does selfish mean? What are the characteristics of a selfish person?

Chapter Thirty-Seven

LET GO OF THE PAST

Therefore, if anyone is in Christ, he is a new creature; the old things have passed away; behold all things are become new.

Sometimes we live in the past, because it's familiar- we know what happened, there are no surprises. By reflecting on the past, you can use this knowledge to change your life for the better.

— 2 CORINTHIANS 5:17

What can you do to let go of your past and move forward? God is ready to help!

What is the sin of covetousness? Give examples of covetousness.

Chapter Thirty-Eight

GIVE IT TO GOD

Be careful for nothing but in everything by prayer and supplication with thanksgiving, let your request be made known unto God.7) And the peace of God which passeth all understanding shall keep your hearts and minds through Christ Jesus.

— PHILIPPIANS 4:6-7

Have your life ever felt out of control? Feeling like there's no hope or help. No matter if it's a health problem, money issues or a bad relationship. Surrendering to God is literally telling God that I'm not big or strong enough to deal with my problem. I need help!

God wants us to have everything in every area of our lives. There are five things the scripture says about giving God our ALL. Your worship Deuteronomy 5:6-10, Your heart

Deuteronomy 10:12-13, Your Tithe Malachi 3:8-12 Your Care 1 Peter 5:7 KJV, Your Trust Proverbs 3 5-6 Take your time and read thru these scriptures.

What is the meaning of selfish? What are examples of being selfish. How can you overcome it?

Chapter Thirty-Nine

SALVATION

That if thou shalt confess with thy mouth the LORD Jesus and shalt believe in thine heart that God hath raised him from the dead, thou shalt be saved. 10) For with the heart man believeth unto righteousness, and with the mouth confession is made unto salvation.

— ROMANS 10:9-10

How does God save you? Read John 3:16, Psalm 34, Romans 3: 23-26 Why does God save? Isaiah 42:5-9 2; Corinthians 5:18 –21

Accepting Jesus Christ as LORD and Savior.

Dear Lord Jesus, I confess that I am a sinner. I believe that you died on the cross for my sins, and you rose again. I ask you Jesus to come into my heart. I accept you now and I confess that you are my LORD and Savior. Help me to live a life pleasing to you! In Jesus' Name!

Psalm 51:10 Create in me a clean heart, O God and renew a right spirit within me.

Chapter Forty

FURTHER STUDY

JESUS PAID FOR IT ALL
SIN PAID PAST MISTAKES PAID
SHAME PAID SLAVERY TO SIN PAID
REJECTION & LONELINESS PAID
SPIRITUAL DEATH PAID

For the wages of sin are death but the gift of God is eternal life in Christ Jesus.

— ROMANS 6:23

Acknowledgments

To my grandchildren: Jalee, Laila, J

To God, who is the head of my life. Who also gave me guidance and direction in writing this book. To my parents Lee A Morgan and Pearl L Morgan, they introduced me to Jesus Christ. They always told me to keep Jesus Christ a priority in my life. To Yanika and A'yeisha keep me appreciating life more.

Made in the USA
Columbia, SC
19 August 2024

40767516R00057